Simply Science

ON THE HIGH SEAS

Gerry Bailey

Illustrations: Steve Boulter & Xact Studio

Diagrams: Karen Radford

AUTHOR: **GERRY BAILEY**

CONSULTANT: **STEVE WAY**

EDITOR: **FELICIA LAW**

ILLUSTRATORS:

STEVE BOULTER

XACT STUDIO

DESIGN: **RALPH PITCHFORD**

ISBN 978-1-906292-17-1
Printed in China

PHOTO CREDITS:

p.5 P & O Ferries.
p.6 Ricardo Manuel Silva de Sousa/Shutterstock Inc.
p.7 (t) Topfoto, (cl) Scott Pehrson/Shutterstock Inc.,
(cr) Graham Prentice/Shutterstock Inc.
p.9 Worldwide Picture Library/Alamy.
p.10-11 Alan Kearney/Photographers Choice/
Getty Images.
p.14 Styve Reineck/Shutterstock Inc.
p.15 Waterways Picture Library.
p.17 (bl) NASA, (br) Goncalo Veloso de
Figueiredo/Shutterstock Inc.
p.19 Susan Harris/Shutterstock Inc.
p.21 SI/Shutterstock Inc.
p.25 Bettmann/Corbis.
p.29 (t) Photri/Topfoto, (b) K.L. Kohn/Shutterstock Inc.

Cover
P & O Ferries.

ON THE HIGH SEAS

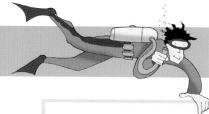

Contents

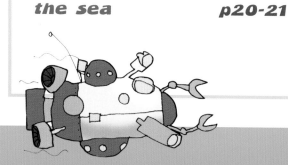

Travelling on water

There are lots of different kinds of waterways. There are seas, of course, and even bigger oceans. Then there are rivers and canals, and lakes to sail across. In fact, there's lots of water to travel on on our planet...

...BUT FIRST YOU NEED A BOAT!

Your boat could be a simple raft

   ...or canoe

...a yacht with big sails

   ...or a large ferry

...or an even bigger liner.

People have travelled on water for thousands of years, to explore, to trade, to fish for food, to go to war or offer peace.

Even with our modern forms of transport, more people than ever travel on water. For example ships like this ferry take people on holiday or to work.

The most important thing about your boat is that it mustn't sink. In other words, it must be able to float. The first boats were logs and rafts. These were made of wood, because wood floats easily on water.

As boat builders learned more about floating and sinking, they started to make bigger ships using wooden planks sealed together with pitch, a kind of tar. The sails were made of skins, cloth or canvas.

Some modern ships are made from a material that's like plastic, called fibreglass. Fibreglass is very light and quite strong.

In the 1800s, engineers built ships made of iron. You'd think iron would be no good for floating because it's so heavy. But the shape and design of the ship made this possible.

Most modern ships are made from huge sheets of steel welded to a steel frame. This forms the hull, decks and main body of the vessel.

Sailing ships, built especially for racing, are made from a man-made material called carbon fibre. This material is lighter than steel but much stronger.

The raft

If a river was too wide, early people couldn't swim across it. They needed a boat.

At first they may have used a log. Then someone had the idea of lashing logs together to build the first rafts.

A raft to cross the river

2. The hunters have to find a way to get to the other side. They might *be able* to paddle across on logs...

1. These prehistoric hunters have found a fine herd of deer. But the deer are on the other side of a river and the river is too wide to swim.

Stronger and safer

The first rafts were probably just logs tied together with strips of animal skin. But later, two logs were added and used as crossbeams. This made the raft more stable.

Reed boat

In Ancient Egypt bundles of reeds were tied together to make rafts. Later, the rafts were curved at the front and back to make boats.

3. But how would they get the deer they had hunted back across the river? If the dead deer fell in, they would become heavy and sink. They needed a way to carry the carcasses across the water.

4. The best way was to make a floating platform from wooden logs. This would carry everyone across the river together - and bring them back.

Floating and sinking

When you put any object into water it will either float or sink. Try it with a few different objects around the house.

Fill a bowl with water and see if you can float:

A TEASPOON?

A BOTTLE CORK?

A PENCIL?

AN APPLE?

Will each sink or float?

What happens depends on the object's weight and its size, These two measurements decide how much space an object takes up – or its density.

It is density that decides if something will float or sink.

Density

All the steel in a big ship has a very high density, so how does it still float?

The steal sheets that the ship is made from may have a high density, far higher than the water it floats in. The steel would just sink straight to the bottom of the water if it was put in the sea before being made into a ship.

Luckily a ship isn't just made up of steel. It contains many air spaces. Air is a lot less dense than water, and the steel and air combined are still less dense than water – and so the ship floats!

A loaded ship "sits" deeper in the water than an unloaded ship because it's got less air spaces within it.

Displacement in the bath

A heavy ship will float IN the water, not on top of it. We say it displaces, or pushes away, the water until the density of the ship and the water are balanced.

Let's say you filled up a bath so it was completely full. Then you lay in it for a few seconds so even your head was covered. The amount of water that spilled onto the floor would be exactly the same as the amount of YOU that took its place – or that you displaced.

The Ancient Greek scientist Archimedes discovered the theory of density while sitting in his bath.

The rudder

The first sailing ships were powered by the wind. You could go where you wanted to – as long as it was in the same direction as the wind was blowing!

If not, it was best to have oars as well as sails. The rowers could then be used to turn the boat. But a rudder would be even better.

A rudder is a flat piece of wood or metal that sticks out from the stern (rear) of the boat. It can be moved from side to side against the flow of the water to help steer the boat.

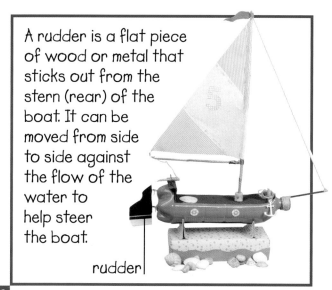

rudder

1. Sailing ships were used to carry rich cargoes of spices and food. But the ships could *be* blown off course in high winds so the cargo would rot before it got to port.

2. Rowers could *be* used to help keep the ship on course. But the ships were huge and needed oars with iron blades for strength – these were heavy.

Steering with a rudder

5. Pushing the rudder left or right turnED the ship one way or the other. If you added a long handle to the rudder, it could then be steered from the deck. This worked well. Now the ship could be steered in most kinds of weather.

3. Also, oars for powering and steering could only be used in calm seas. Rough, stormy waves would snap them in pieces.

4. But a kind of oar, or rudder, fixed to the rear of the ship could use the flow of water around it to help steer the ship, or at least keep it in a straight line.

Along the canal

During the 1800s, new factories in Britain poured out their products to be transported to cities and to sea ports. There was so much to be carried that the road system couldn't cope. So engineers had to dig canals. These man-made rivers helped keep things moving.

Canals are even cut through high rocks so that large ships can find a short cut to the sea.

Soon, many countries had their own canal networks to help transport products such as coal and cloth. Flat-bottomed boats, called barges, moved under steam power, or were sometimes pulled along by horses.

5. An instrument called an astrolabe was an invention that helped make the vital calculation. It was a disc marked with a scale of 360 degrees and a moveable pointer attached to the centre. Navigators would look at stars and measure in degrees how high the stars were above the horizon. By comparing this with a land chart of the same star positions, they could tell where they were.

The astrolabe

Early sailors could work out where they were as long as they could see the shore. But in open water, they were in trouble. That is, until the astrolabe was invented. It helped navigators make accurate measurements using points in the night sky.

An astrolabe was an instrument used by navigators to measure how high the sun, a planet or a star is above the horizon.

angle   horizon

Seas and oceans

When the first sailors looked out over the ocean, they could see that the horizon was a curved shape. They could see the waters might go on and on forever - even to the edge of the world!

They didn't know just how large the oceans actually were. But that didn't stop them using the oceans for trade and transport.

If we keep near the coast, we can't go wrong.

Mighty oceans

In fact, the oceans cover a lot of space on our planet - 71% or nearly three-quarters of it. There are five main oceans.

Pacific Ocean

The oceans may look still when you see them on a map, but they are all moving. They move round the world as currents, as rising tides and in waves.

Seas are smaller areas of water than oceans. There are many seas across the globe, including the Red Sea and the Yellow Sea. Bays and gulfs are smaller areas of water that lie around the coasts.

Arctic Ocean

Atlantic Ocean

Pacific Ocean

Indian Ocean

Antarctic Ocean

All oceans are made up of salt water. Salt that is found in the soil and rocks on land is washed into the sea by heavy rains and strong waves.

Travelling under the sea

What lies under the deep oceans has always excited explorers and scientists. But until the first underwater transport machines were invented, people could only guess at the wonders that lay there.

Diving suit

In a diving suit, I can do almost as well as a fish.

Really skilled divers could hold their breath for many minutes while they explored the sea bed close to shore. Then they had to come up again. They couldn't breathe for long underwater. They tried to find a way of taking air with them. And as a result, the first diving suit was invented.

Early diving suits were heavy and difficult to move in. They had long tubes down which the air flowed from a boat on the surface. Later, the divers wanted something lighter that let them swim freely. The answer was SCUBA, or self-contained underwater breathing apparatus. Now you could carry your own supply of air in a tank fastened onto your back.

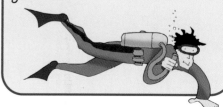

Submersible

Smaller submarines, known as submersibles, were developed for exploration. They had strong shells, or hulls, because they descended far down into deep water that would have crushed a normal submarine.

Submarine

The first underwater craft were submarines. They were actually 'mini warships' that could stalk enemy ships under the water and then shoot torpedoes at them. Modern nuclear submarines can stay underwater for months.

This modern Russian submarine, powered by diesel-electricity, can move very quietly in fairly shallow waters.

Submarine inventors

A submarine is a ship that can travel under the water as well as on top of it. It has tanks inside that fill with water to make it sink. The tanks are emptied when the submarine needs to surface again.

Hiding underwater

1. In 1620, a Dutch scientist called Cornelius van Drebbel, demonstrated an underwater craft. It was actually just a rowing boat covered in waterproof animal skins.

2. During the American Revolution, David Bushnell, a student, designed a one-man attack submarine called the 'Turtle'. It hung from the bottom of a boat.

How do submarines work?

To dive:

1. Open the vents and the flood openings.
2. The sub will sink as the ballast tanks fill with water.

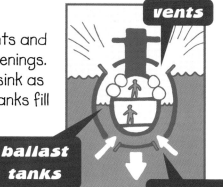

vents

ballast tanks

flood openings

To surface:

1. Close the vents.
2. Empty the ballast tanks of water by blowing air into them from the air tanks.

air tanks

---

3. Then another American, Robert Fulton, built a copper-covered sub that could actually sink ships. But it was over six metres long - and no-one showed much interest in it!

4. In 1889, the Irishman John Holland, launched a 16-metre sub powered by petrol and electricity. Its streamlined shape helped it move quickly and silently through the water.

5. It took several inventors to come up with the periscope. This uses mirrors and is raised to the surface to spy out any ships sailing nearby.

The bathyscaphe

A bathyscaphe is a kind of craft that can dive deep below the ocean's surface. It is used mostly for exploring the deepest caverns of the ocean bed.

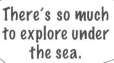

There's so much to explore under the sea.

Up and down in deep waters

1. The bathysphere was invented to protect divers from the heavy water pressure at the bottom of the sea.
Pressure like this can squeeze the life out of you!

2. The first bathysphere had to be attached to a boat so divers couldn't explore very far – only what was underneath them. They wanted to go deeper. But they would need a very long chain to be lowered and pulled back up again.

A 2-part solution

The modern bathyscaphe is a sphere, or large ball, made of very thick steel. It's attached to a long hull filled with gasoline. The gasoline helps it to float.

hull filled with gasoline

sphere

3. Auguste Piccard designed an airtight sphere fitted beneath a boat-shaped hull. It didn't need to be attached to anything.

4. Piccard used gasoline instead of water as ballast, or weight, in the hull. That made the new bathyscaphe float. The bathyscaphe could descend to over 10 kilometres.

Crawling along the bottom

1. Scientists needed a small submarine to explore the sea bed. It had to carry three or four divers and be able to stay underwater for days rather than hours.

2. The submersible would need a strong hull to protect the divers. It also needed to carry extra equipment to help divers do different jobs underwater.

3. Small underwater craft that were attached to a ship could dive to around 300 metres. But there were much deeper places on the ocean floor that scientists wanted to explore.

4. In 1977 ocean explorer, Robert Ballard, and his team used a submersible to find amazing hot water vents, or volcanic holes, on the ocean floor. A whole new world of living things, including strange worms, lived around the vents.

The submersible

A submersible is an underwater boat that can move along the sea bed. It's useful for exploring and taking photographs.

5. With lights, cameras and lots of action the submersible continues to help divers map out the seabed and create the geography of the oceans.

A submersible uses its own engines for power so it can move easily along the bottom of the sea. Submersibles often have cameras and floodlights to help the divers see and to light the area around so pictures can be taken. Some have mechanical arms that can pick up samples from the sea floor.

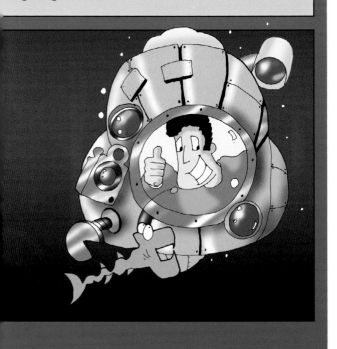

Fighting ships

It didn't take long before armies realised how useful ships could be in helping to win a war. They could be used to transport fighting men, but, with a large cannon on board, they could also be used to blow other ships out of the water.

Galleon

The galleon was used by the Spanish in the 1500s to transport gold from South America. It was a big ship and not very easy to sail. It had cannon below and above deck.

Trireme

Ancient Greek navies used a ship that had one mast and rows of oars. Slaves pulled the oars to power the ships. A ship with three banks of oars was called a trireme. Usually there was a battering ram at the front of it.

Aircraft carrier

An aircraft carrier is one of the largest fighting ships. It has to carry fighter-bombers in its hold and has a short runway on deck where the planes can take off and land.

Hunter-killer submarine

These nuclear submarines are designed to hunt down and destroy shipping or enemy submarines. Some carry nuclear warheads.

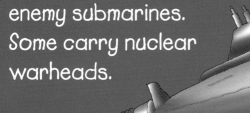

Battleship

A battleship is a large warship that carries heavy guns. Its guns can be aimed at other ships, or at targets on land.

Sea transport Quiz

1. Who used a boat made from bundles of reeds tied together?

_____

2. What is the name of the flat blade attached to the stern of a boat that helps steer it?

_____

3. Which animal can help pull a barge?

_____

4. Which instrument helped sailors steer by the stars?

_____

5. Name an ocean that begins with P.

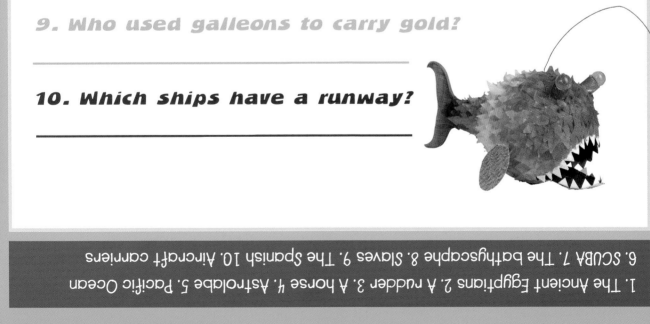

6. What is the short name for self-contained underwter breathing apparatus?

_____

7. What kind of sea craft did Auguste Piccard invent?

_____

8. Who powered a trireme?

_____

9. Who used galleons to carry gold?

_____

10. Which ships have a runway?

_____

1. The Ancient Egyptians 2. A rudder 3. A horse 4. Astrolabe 5. Pacific Ocean 6. SCUBA 7. The bathyscaphe 8. Slaves 9. The Spanish 10. Aircraft carriers

31

Index